Your Retirement Roadmap

Common Sense Strategies To Take You To and Through Retirement

Zach B. Gray, CRPC

Your Retirement Roadmap
Printed by:
Independent Publishing
Copyright © 2017, Zach Gray
Published in the United States of America
ISBN: 9781976424014
No parts of this publication may be reproduced without correct attribution to the author of this book.

Zach Gray is a licensed insurance agent and is registered as an Investment Adviser Representative. Rooted Wealth Advisors is an independent financial services firm that helps individuals create retirement strategies using a variety of investment and insurance products to custom suit their needs and objectives. Investment advisory services offered only by duly registered individuals through Rooted Wealth Advisors, Inc.

The contents of this book are provided for informational purposes only and are not intended to serve as the basis for any financial decisions. Any tax, legal or estate planning information is general in nature. It should not be construed as legal or tax advice. Always consult an attorney or tax professional regarding the applicability of this information to your unique situation.

Information presented is believed to be factual and up-to-date, but we do not guarantee its accuracy and it should not be regarded as a complete analysis of the subjects discussed. All expressions of opinion are those of the author as of the date of publication and are subject to change. Content should not be construed as personalized investment advice nor should it be interpreted as an offer to buy or sell any securities mentioned. A financial advisor should be consulted before implementing any of the strategies presented.

Investing involves risk, including the potential loss of principal. No investment strategy can guarantee a profit or protect against loss in periods of declining values. Any references to protection benefit or guaranteed/lifetime income streams refer only to fixed insurance products, not securities or investment products. Insurance and annuity product guarantees are backed by the financial strength and claims-paying ability of the issuing insurance company.

Rooted Wealth Advisors is not related to, endorsed by, nor connected with and not approved by any government agency or organization. For information regarding your Social Security benefits, you are encouraged to speak to your local Social Security Administration office or visit the Social Security Administration website at www.ssa.gov

Here's What's Inside...

Introduction 1

Why Don't More People Know How to
Prepare for Retirement? 3

The Retirement Roadmap 7

Threat #1: Outliving Their Money 8

Threat #2: Market Volatility Risk 11

Threat #3: Taxes 14

Threat #4: Social Security 19

Threat #5: Health Care 22

Threat #6: Plan – There Is
No Need to Fight 27

The Common Mistakes
Made In Retirement 29

Here's How to Create Your
Retirement Roadmap 39

Introduction

Your Retirement Roadmap!

I got my start in the financial services industry after seeing firsthand what poor planning can do.

When I was just getting out of college, my grandparents on both sides of my family were starting their retirement. Unfortunately, soon after they moved out of their steady jobs, both sets of grandparents were met with financial curveballs. I watched as both sides of the family had to deal with the issues that retirement was throwing at them, issues that they hadn't planned for.

One of the many results of this lack of planning was that my father's mother, who is in her 80s, still works part time to this day to supplement her income. Watching my grandparents struggle because of some issues they ran into early in retirement was like a call to action for my career path.

Just like what I observed through my family's experiences, there are so many things that can derail a retirement; everyone should have the information I share in this book, so they can put a proper plan in place to retire prepared. No one wants to make mistakes with retirement after working all those years to do so. No one wants to be a burden to their kids. When something happens that we don't plan for, all too often the result is having to live extremely frugally, which no one wants for their loved ones in the sunset of their life.

Unfortunately, it seems there simply isn't a lot of this information available to folks and presented in a way in which you don't get confused, frustrated, or overwhelmed. The financial industry is filled with a lot of jargon and confusing terms, which is what drove me to want to write this book.

I hope this book educates you on the importance of getting started with your retirement plan and not leaving it for another day. I hope this book inspires you to take the first step, as that is often the most difficult.

If I can affect your family in a positive way, and help you avoid some of the threats or potholes to your retirement, then this book will have done its job.

Enjoy the book!

To Your Financial Future!

Zach Gray

Why Don't More People Know How to Prepare for Retirement?

In my office, Root Wealth Advisors, I meet with people who are planning to retire and those who are already retired to help them figure out one basic thing. We may talk about many financial products, and we may look over charts and graphs and crunch some numbers, but a lot of it comes down to trying to help them figure out a plan for receiving income in retirement.

This may seem like a simple proposition, but many of the people I meet in my office are unprepared, and haven't thought the variables through.

Why is that?

It can really be boiled down to one word: procrastination. We're all guilty of this. I believe that is, without question, the No. 1 reason we have the issues that we do when it comes to planning for our retirement. One of the reasons we fail to prepare is that for a lot of people, doing financial planning is simply not fun. In my experience, I have found that we spend more time over the course of our lifetime planning vacations than we do planning our retirements. That's eye opening, but it's the sad truth.

So what is the reason behind the procrastination? Why do we think people put it off?

To be frank, I think it's because doing a proper financial plan takes work, and, for many people, it's daunting. Retirement planning is something that not everyone understands fully, and we tend to procrastinate on things we don't feel confident about. It's a lot like getting in shape. When we start a new year one of the most common resolutions is, "I'm going to get back into shape."

We've all seen the storylines or the statistics when it comes to gym memberships; trying to get back into the shape of our teenage years just simply doesn't happen. It takes time and it's not easy. If it was, we'd all be at our ideal weight. We'd all eat better if it were easy to do. You have to plan ahead and find healthy food recipes and source the ingredients. It's a heck of a lot easier to cruise through the fast-food line and grab a cheeseburger. With retirement planning, often our retirement is so far off in the future, it's easier to just deal with all the things we have on our plate today rather than sit down and work out all that needs to go into a successful retirement plan for tomorrow.

Also, retirement—both the reality and the preparation for it—is ever changing. Our grandparents probably worked for 40 years for the same company and when they got close to the end, they threw them a big party and they gave them a gold watch and they also gave them a big benefit called a pension. It was easier planning to retire 20 years ago. Back then, you worked for a certain number of years, and you were guaranteed a certain amount of money. It took a lot of the advance planning off of our table.

However, that's not the case anymore. That landscape has changed in a big way and that's one reason it also gets a little daunting. Years ago, the planning was a lot easier and there are other things to factor in, today we are living longer. So now, our money has to last longer than previous generations. Factor in that we have greater market volatility, it seems like any given week the stock market tickers are up and then down, and that puts a new pressure on our retirement planning. All of these risks have started to play a lot more into our retirement picture.

This book is titled *Your Retirement Roadmap* for a reason: to try to lay out some of the pitfalls and speed bumps that people are going to encounter along the way while planning for retirement. It will also outline situations to steer away from while in retirement.

Another reason people procrastinate about preparing for retirement? The basic financial material that goes into this type of planning simply isn't always learned. Some schools have financial literacy programs that cover varying degrees of subjects, but many do not. And as we grow into adulthood, life oftentimes gets in the way of mastering these concepts. We get busy with activities, with kids, with jobs, with all the day-to-day work of life, and this concern for retirement planning is often left for another day.

A lot of times, we'll sit down with a client, they'll simply say, "Hey, we did the best we could with what we knew." Sometimes, it works out, and then sometimes, you wish that things would have maybe been done a little differently. With a little bit of guidance, we can sure help those who have some of those questions when it comes to retirement and we can try to make things a little bit easier for them going forward.

The Retirement Roadmap

When it comes to creating your own roadmap for retirement, it's important to remember that there are a lot of different things that can come someone's way in retirement. We don't have a crystal ball, so we don't know always exactly what's coming. However, we tend to see some of the same major wrong turns or threats people encounter in their retirement.

If you see retirement as a journey, part of mapping it out is knowing where you are and where you want to be. Any good map is about avoiding obstacles, figuring out where you want to make stops along the way, and knowing when to take the marked detour!

Often, when we speak to a group of people and we ask them for their feedback about what their biggest fears or concerns are when it comes to retirement. The conversation almost always circles back the same concerns or topics, many of which provide those metaphorical forks in the road that can be challenging even for today's most advanced GPS technologies. The following topics are some of the most frequently cited concerns when people think about retirement.

Threat #1: Outliving Their Money

The first concern I see a lot is fear of outliving their money. We touched upon the fact that retirement is a lot different today than what it was years ago, and that it's safe to say this is not your daddy's retirement, let alone your granddaddy's retirement.

To see the proof of that statement, I would instruct you, dear reader, to ask yourself the question, "Have you been working for the same company your entire life?" The overwhelming majority of those who read this book are going to answer, "No." Are readers going to get the gold watch and, more importantly, the pension at the end of their time working for that particular company? The answer there is probably going to be no. That changed in a big way back in the 70s when Congress enacted the Employee Retirement Income Security Act, or ERISA. Many legislators saw ERISA as a way to help strengthen pensions, but one major effect was that it really touched upon a section of the tax code that is the main reason that we have such a prevalent 401(k) world.

It took a lot of pressure off of the companies and it put it in the hands of the investors or of the people who worked there. With a defined-benefit plan like a pension, you had an annual income you could count on, so you knew you wouldn't run out of money. Yet, here are the stats from CNN Money:

"The percentage of workers in the private sector whose only retirement account is a defined benefit pension plan is now 4%, down from 60% in the early 1980s."[1]

As far as outliving our money is concerned, do you think the decline of pensions has made a difference? I'd say yes.

That is one of the biggest things that is a concern to clients. It ties into another speed bump, if you will, and that would be a market risk in retirement.

One must ask themselves, if we had another market decline like we did in 2008, how does that affect my retirement picture? Oftentimes, creating our own stream of income can be one of the best ways to address this concern.

There are many ways to create your own income stream. One way is to take market risk off the table by buying a fixed index annuity. This can be especially helpful to cover necessities and reoccurring expenses, and might be a good option for you to consider. What is an annuity?

---

[1] CNN Money. 2017. "Ultimate Guide to Retirement: Just How Common Are Defined Benefit Plans?"
http://money.cnn.com/retirement/guide/pensions_basics.mon eymag/index7.htm?iid=EL. Accessed Aug. 2, 2017.

An annuity is a contract you purchase from an insurance company. For the premium you pay, you receive certain fixed and/or variable interest crediting options able to compound tax deferred until withdrawn. When you are ready to receive income distributions, this vehicle offers a variety of guaranteed payout options — some even for life. To give the quick definition of a fixed index annuity, then, I'll quote USA Today.

"A fixed index annuity is a fixed annuity that, according to the Insured Retirement Institute's report, credits a minimum guaranteed rate of interest over a fixed number of years, plus additional interest that may be credited based on the percentage change in the value of a broad market index."[2]

---

[2] Robert Powell. Aug. 19, 2015. USA Today. "Retirement: Pros and Cons of Fixed-Index Annuities."
https://www.usatoday.com/story/money/columnist/powell/2015/08/13/retirement-pros-and-cons-fixed-income-annuities/30626141/. Accessed Aug. 2, 2017.

Threat #2: Market Volatility Risk

Threat 1 leads right into Threat 2. Someone can grow their money over the course of time and, while we may not pay that much attention to those accounts as we go up the mountain, it starts to matter to us very much as we reach the peak and start thinking about the trek back down, so to speak.

If our account value goes up, down, or flat; it's all about what that closing balance is at the end of the day.

We're working toward retirement and trying to help grow our assets for retirement. If we lose a little bit of money early on, it doesn't matter as much if that's a jagged step up the mountain because, after all, what really matters is what the total amount is. It can be a "rocky road," but, in our working years, as long as we are still accumulating, we don't worry quite as much as when we are in retirement and we are starting to use those savings for income.

The point of my story is that if we end up in a situation where we have some bad years early on in retirement, now we're putting our retirement in jeopardy.

When we approach retirement, we look at this as coming back down the mountain. If you have a big down market right when you are retiring, right when you are taking some money out of your market accounts, it can be a big problem. We call this sequence of return risk. What it can end up doing is depleting our money faster if we end up having some bad years early on in retirement. The sequence of return risk is a big deal when it comes to someone's retirement, because if we're losing money *and* we're pulling money out, we're expediting those losses even faster, and that can put someone's retirement in jeopardy.

If we see major market swings shortly before someone's retirement or shortly after, we can have some harsh blows to our retirement portfolio. As of the writing of this book, we're at all-time highs, as far as market levels are concerned. Yet, that is not always the case. Those retiring closer to 2008, in many cases, had to delay retirement or lower their lifestyle expectations because of the impact on their portfolios.

Fortunately, there are some things we can do to help mitigate losses.

There are ways to help grow your money over time. One quick step you can take is to apply "The Rule of 100" to your investment picture. Simply take 100, subtract your age, and the number remaining should be the approximate percentage of your portfolio that should be held in equities/stocks. The other portion of the portfolio should be in something more conservative. These types of financial products are designed to offer a layer of protection to help you lessen the chance of losses during market downturns.

By taking a look at the following example, you will see the importance of the sequence of returns. On the way up, the returns are the same as the way down, but see what impact ultimately is in the distribution phase of this example:

Investor A Initial Investment: $100,000 $5,000/yr Withdrawls at Year End		Investor B Initial Investment: $100,000 $5,000/yr Withdrawls at Year End	
Return	Year-end Value	Return	Year-end Value
-9.10	$85,900.00	13.69	$108,690
-11.89	$70,686.49	32.39	$138,895
-22.10	$50,064.78	16.00	$156,118
28.68	$59,423.35	2.11	$154,412
10.88	$60,888.61	15.06	$172,666
4.91	$58,878.25	26.46	$213,354
15.79	$63,175.12	-37.00	$129,413
5.49	$61,643.43	5.49	$131,518
-37.00	$33,835.36	15.79	$147,284
26.46	$37,788.20	4.91	$149,516
15.06	$38,479.10	10.88	$160,783
2.11	$34,291.01	28.68	$201,896
16.00	$34,777.57	-22.10	$152,277
32.39	$41,042.03	-11.89	$129,171
13.69	$41,660.69	-9.10	$112,417
6.09% Average Annual Return		6.09% Average Annual Return	

This example is for illustration purposes only and does not represent any specific product or investment, nor does it reflect the deduction of investment fees or taxes.

Threat #3: Taxes

Whether I am speaking across the country or am at one of my local seminars, I typically ask the audience, "Who thinks taxes are going to go down in the future?" By an overwhelming majority, people think taxes are going to go up, and I tend to agree with that. But when I ask them how many of their financial advisors have addressed this issue when it comes to their retirement picture, rarely any heads are nodding in agreement.

I'll often follow up with, "How high do you think they're going to be able to go up?" They find it ironic that the highest bracket in the United States' history is 94 percent. That was years ago, at the tail end of the World War II. Our highest tax bracket today is 39.6 percent, which is a far cry from 94 percent.[3][4] It makes today's brackets look pretty good. You don't have to go back that far in history to find out that taxes were a fair amount higher.

---

[3] Jeff Haden. CBS News. Dec. 7, 2011. "How Would You Feel About a 94% Tax Rate?"
http://www.cbsnews.com/news/how-would-you-feel-about-a-94-tax-rate/. Accessed Aug. 2, 2017.

[4] Tina Orem. NerdWallet. May 14, 2017. "2017 Federal Income Tax Brackets."
https://www.nerdwallet.com/blog/taxes/federal-income-tax-brackets/. Accessed Aug. 2, 2017.

For example, the highest marginal tax rate didn't drop below 70 percent until the 80s.[5] That being said, it may change someone's prerogative about how bad they think taxes are today. We often feel that taxes are as bad as they've ever been, but in all reality, they're probably good. It might make you think a little bit about taking it into account how much money you might really be saving with your IRA or 401(k). For example, if someone put $15,000 a year into a 401(k) and they were in a 33 percent effective tax bracket, that means that they would be deferring about $5,000 a year in taxes, 1/3 of $15,000 is $5,000.

If they did that for 15 years, they would have put in $225,000 into that 401(k) fund. Of course, you'd hope that those funds are growing over the course of time, so if we net out a hypothetical 7 percent annual rate of return, that $225,000 has grown over the course of that time to $403,000, and 15 years times a $5,000–a-year tax deferral ends up being about $75,000 saved in taxes.

This is best shown in an illustration designed by a friend and colleague of mine, Marty Ruby, FSA. Marty is the CEO of Stonewood Financial based out of Louisville, Kentucky. Marty's background as an actuary and former CEO of Integrity Life Insurance has given him the knowledge and understanding to

---

[5] Jeff Haden. CBS News. Dec. 7, 2011. "How Would You Feel About a 94% Tax Rate?"
http://www.cbsnews.com/news/how-would-you-feel-about-a-94-tax-rate/. Accessed Aug. 2, 2017.

create the following illustration. In my opinion, he captures it best.

Taxes: The Reality of Tax Deferral

Because tax-deferred financial vehicles require participants to ultimately pay income tax on contributed assets *and* earned interest, it's important to consider what role taxes may play in your retirement income strategy. Below is a hypothetical example of a tax-deferred account, like an IRA. This example shows the taxes deferred at the time of contribution, and the taxes owed at the time of withdrawal.

For this example, we've assumed an individual in the 33% tax bracket contributes $15,000 annually for 15 years with a 7% net annual growth rate into a tax-deferred asset, like a 401(k) or IRA, and that his tax bracket stays the same during retirement.

This example doesn't consider every product or feature of tax-deferred accounts and is for illustrative purposes only. It should not be deemed a representation of past or future results, and is no guarantee of return or future performance. Your tax bracket may be lower or higher in retirement, unlike this hypothetical example. Tax-free distributions are accessed through the use of policy loans and withdrawals through a life insurance contract. Accessing these funds will reduce available cash values and death benefits and may cause the policy to lapse. Additional premium payments may be required to keep the policy in force. In the event of a lapse, outstanding policy loans in excess of unrecovered cost basis will be subject to ordinary income tax. **This information is not intended to provide tax, legal, or investment advice. Be sure to speak with qualified professionals before making any decisions about your personal situation.**

When we start thinking about withdrawals from that particular account, let's say that we're going to withdraw about $32,500 for 25 years, and also those dollars would be continuously growing as we take the money out, if we stayed in the similar tax bracket—which, of course, the argument is, "What will be in the same tax bracket or will we not be in the same tax bracket?"—but if we stayed in the 33 percent effective tax range out of that $32,500, we'd be paying $10,750 in taxes with each year.

Over the course of time, we're going take out $806,250 in withdrawals over 25 years. Out of that money, if we stay in that 33 percent effective tax bracket, then we've paid about $268,750 in taxes. We've deferred $75,000 and we've ended up having to pay $268,000.

Now you may be thinking to yourself, I will be in a lower tax environment in retirement simply because I won't be working. But, do you really want to take a pay cut in retirement? Not many people do. Many actually need more in retirement to travel the way they have always wanted, or to do the bucket list items they have had in mind.

It really gets your mind turning about how to handle those 401(k)s or those IRAs and things of that nature because taxes are important when it comes to retirement. They are particularly important to keep in mind when it comes to Social Security. It's one of the things that is a speed bump, or something to look out for, when it comes to someone's retirement. We often develop a strategy to help our clients position their assets for tax efficiency. This can be very beneficial for not only their retirement, but for the next generation, as well. We'll cover this a little more in-depth in coming chapters.

Threat #4: Social Security

Social Security is always a topic of conversation when it comes to retirement. Social Security is affected primarily by two major things. No. 1 is when you choose to take it and which filing option to select. If we had a crystal ball, we would know exactly when to take it, because Social Security works similar to a pension in that it stops paying benefits when you pass away. There are special considerations for spouses who are collecting when one of them passes away.

The second thing that affects Social Security income comes in the form of provisional income. Provisional income is the income that tells us how much of our Social Security becomes taxed. This will include income coming from a taxable or being realized from a tax-deferred state. Think of a taxable bucket as resembling your bank account—your savings account, for example—and you're going to get a small 1099 each year. This includes any mutual funds or stocks or bonds that you have, with nonqualified money, money market accounts, things of that nature—even income, whether that's part-time or full-time income. Provisional income is also affected by anything coming out of a tax-deferred bucket of money. By a tax-deferred bucket, we mean things like a 401(k) or an IRA or a 403(b) or a SEP plan, you get the idea. That's the bucket of money for which we've been kicking the taxes further down the road.

At the end of the day, Social Security may be taxed because provisional income equates to 50 percent of someone's Social Security benefits they receive plus any additional income they get out of those two buckets of money, that is, out of that taxable bucket or that tax-deferred bucket. If a grand total—all those dollars out of 50 percent of that Social Security income plus any of those dollars out of those two buckets of money—ends up being less than $32,000 for married filing jointly, for example, 0 percent is taxed (as of the 2017 writing of this book).

The next step in 2017 is $32,000 to $44,000—and that's a quite a big jump—at which point, 50 percent of your total household Social Security becomes taxable. The last step is anything over $44,000-worth of income, where 85 percent of your Social Security would become taxable. It's important to note that this is a "married filing joint" example; single tax payers have a reduced limit.

It's very important to properly time out when to take Social Security, but it's also very important to figure out how provisional income is going to affect Social Security, because that is going to be a significant factor in how much of your Social Security money you truly end up being able to keep.

This is yet another supporting argument to getting some of your money into my favorite bucket, the third bucket, the tax-free bucket. Ultimately, distributions from this bucket are not taxable and do not have an effect on this provisional income formula. We run the numbers for clients and prospects day in and day out, and if someone can help their Social Security from being taxed, they likely can have their assets last five to seven years longer in retirement.

Threat #5: Health Care

Another issue where often I see people make wrong turns in their retirement is health care. Health care is by far the number one cost in someone's retirement today. I'll often ask, "What's the biggest bill you're going to pay in retirement?" People throw out things like utilities or travel, and things of that nature, but the overwhelming true answer is health care. In fact, it's not even close to the others. It's pretty eye-opening. According to the Health View: 2017 Healthcare Cost Data Report, a 65-year-old couple will spend somewhere around $321,994 on health care.[6] Let that sink in.

Three hundred, twenty-one thousand, nine hundred ninety four dollars! And that's just for any Medicare Part B premiums, anything that falls in the donut hole of Medicare such as deductibles and co-pays as described by hvsfinancial.com.

According to that same report, if they were included that number is expected to grow to $404,253! That's from today's dollars, if there were no inflation that ever hit. If we inflate those dollars—it's roughly

---

[6] HealthView Services. 2017. "2017 Retirement Health Care Costs Data Report." http://www.hvsfinancial.com/2017-retirement-health-care-costs-data-report/. Accessed Aug. 2, 2017.

about 3 percent—that means someone's going to spend somewhere around $607,662 in retirement just on health care premiums and deductibles and vision and hearing coverage that might not be covered by Medicare. It's important to note these costs, because those are things that we must plan for. So many times people say, "As soon as I get to 65, health care is going to become much less of a worry because I'm going to get on Medicare." It's not quite as easy as that answer. Those figures also don't consider what maybe one of the biggest health care cost risks out there, and that comes in the form of long-term care.

My step-grandmother has Parkinson's disease, and she's been suffering from it for quite some time. About a decade ago, my grandfather could no longer care for her properly at home, so he had to seek out skilled care for her and he has been paying out of pocket ever since. As of the writing of this book, he's paying approximately $8,000 a month out of pocket, and that's just for the skilled care portion of what she needs. That doesn't factor in some of the health care costs we were talking about before when it came to shortfalls in Medicare and things of that nature. He's been paying that for a decade, and it's nearly a million dollars in costs associated with health care, but specifically that million dollars is associated solely with the cost of her long-term care.

This was a pitfall in his retirement strategy to say the least. It was nothing my grandfather saw coming at such an early age, and when my grandmother's diagnosis took shape there was no getting such insurance. Once a couple hits the age of 65, there's a 70 percent chance they're going to need long-term care.[7]

If we take that into account, that's a pretty high risk for someone who's likely just entering retirement or is at least thinking about retirement.

According to a survey done by Genworth in April of 2016, the national average for a private room in a skilled care facility is $7,698; just shy of $250/day.[8] The last piece of that equation is how long you will need such care. According to LongTermCare.gov, the average need for care is about three years. Women need an average of 3.7 years of care, while men need an average of 2.2 years. If that weren't enough, 20 percent of the people turning 65 today will need more than five years' worth of care![9]

If we play those numbers out for two people, a 65-year-old couple, let's just say that there's a 70 percent chance that they're going to need long-term care and we use $200 a day, 365 days in a year for let's say

---

[7] LongTermCare.gov. 2017. "Who Needs Care?" https://longtermcare.acl.gov/the-basics/who-needs-care.html. Accessed Aug. 2, 2017.
[8] Genworth Financial. 2016. "2016 Cost of Care Survey." https://www.genworth.com/about-us/industry-expertise/cost-of-care.html. Accessed Aug. 2, 2017.
[9] LongTermCare.gov. 2017. "Who Needs Care?" https://longtermcare.acl.gov/the-basics/who-needs-care.html. Accessed Aug. 2, 2017.

three years. That becomes a cost of about $306,600. Two people, 70 percent chance, $200 a day, 365 days in a year, and a three-year need, $306,600.

If we inflate that at roughly 3 percent, in 20 years, that number grows to $586,919, so it really goes to show you that this can be a big detriment to someone's retirement and it's typically something that very few people have thought about.

Why is it so seldom that people prepare for these eventualities? I think it stems back to how we started the book. It's one of those things that's tough to think about. No one wants to think about being in a nursing home. The sad truth is that many of us are going to need some sort of skilled nursing care. We are going to need assistance late in life, and that's something that needs to be planned for. Years ago, we might say, "My daughter would be the one who helps with that care," or, "Our kids are going to be the ones who help with that care." We also know that, in today's world, a lot of times we're looking at a two-income family. The costs of long-term care, well, they keep escalating, especially with the baby boom generation on the brink of such care.

When we think about health care, we have to think about two particular things.

No. 1, what's our cost of health care look like? Secondly, what's the cost of long-term care? And then we have to realize that someone will have to pay for those costs.

I guess another factor to point out is, when it comes to health care costs and health care needs, do we want to be a burden to our children, or to the next generation? Can they take care of us? You know, my grandfather's example is something that is eye-opening, but he was really in pretty good health when his wife started needing care. He just did not have the facility nor did he have the skill, or even just the knowledge to take care of that disease. So, to leave this chapter with a thought, preparing for the costs of all our health care needs in retirement is about more than just ourselves and our lives.

Threat #6: Plan – There Is No Need to Fight

The last threat we discussed takes us right into the finale. This roadmap is largely focused on simply planning. That may conjure up a very broad and diverse concept, but I'm thinking of planning along the lines of making sure that wills are updated and making sure that things are properly documented and making sure that our true desires are going to be carried out when we're no longer here.

"Failing to plan, is planning to fail." We've all seen way too many families in a situation where things get torn apart when the older generation, the father or the mother, passes away or needs care. You know, who's going to be responsible for taking care of Mom and Dad if they haven't planned for that in their retirement? Then, does it all become one child's burden or responsibility? How is that handled by others going forward?

You know, one of the first questions I ask a client is, "Do you have a will in place?" It doesn't matter if they're 80 years old or if they're 20 years old. How about a trust? And if so, did that trust get properly funded?

We do not know when our last day is going to be; we don't have that crystal ball. If we don't know when that day is, we definitely need to take some time and make sure that we have some sort of plan in place for our last day. I believe it's part of my job to try to make sure we put a roadmap in place to help navigate all these twists and turns, all these different issues that might pop up along the road to retirement.

There's one thing we can do, and that is putting some of those final planning pieces in place. It's important for someone to make sure that it's documented. We've just seen way too many families be torn apart because some of those burdens or those decisions that are left to the next generation.

Common Mistakes Made In Retirement

There is no single way to do retirement "right." After all, what appeals to one retiree won't necessarily be exciting to another. However, I think we can all observe in the world around us that there are certainly ways to get retirement "wrong."

One of the pieces that I see a lot of problems with is people who don't try to plan for, or at least be cognizant of, the need for long-term care. Obviously, if my grandfather could go back in time and buy long-term-care insurance coverage for my step-grandmother, I'm sure that would be one of the first places he would put his money—into a contract like that. We often hear some of the financial gurus say that you should wait until 50. I've heard more than one financial talking head say that's the prime age to buy a long-term care policy of some kind.

The truth of the matter is that if you end up being 49 and need double-knee surgery or you need back surgery, and you're planning on waiting until that magic age of 50 to apply for such coverage, just those types of surgeries, nothing major health related, can cause issues when it comes to trying to apply and get a long-term care contract. My grandfather is a case in point for that. He says all the time, "I was just waiting to get to a little bit later point in our life. I never thought in a million years we would ever need to worry about that so early on." Obviously, if he could change it and start planning for that, he could have been a lot happier during retirement and had more financial independence.

That thought brings another to mind. I often hear that purchasing permanent life insurance is a bad financial choice. The reason I say the above topic brings this to mind is that permanent life insurance contracts, also known as cash value insurance, can have their fair share of benefits in addition to the death benefit, such as providing an alternative for paying for long term care expenses. Many people do not know that some "accelerated benefits" such as chronic or critical care riders exist on these types of policies.

Also, they can be a great way to transfer wealth tax-free upon death, and can have several tax advantages while someone is alive, as well. Cash value accumulation typically accrues free of tax, and loans against these types of contracts are typically tax-free as long as the policy does not terminate before the death of the insured. Of course, there are many things to consider when deciding if a permanent life contract is the right decision. Among those considerations are age, the cost of insurance, and how to properly manage the contract to realize its intended tax benefits, or simply seeing if someone is healthy enough to qualify through underwriting. I'm simply proposing that someone not discount permanent life insurance altogether. There are several advantages to many of these policies.

To circle the wagons back to where I started, with talking about pitfalls or things that we're trying to work around when it comes to someone's retirement and doing that through our roadmap-type process, is that outliving someone's money is something that, you know, is a very big concern. People are living, much, much longer.

When Social Security started out in the 1940s, you originally had to be 65 years of age to start benefits, as you will see on the social security website.[10] That's because the average age of death at that point in time was 62. Not only that, but we had 42 people in the workforce for every one recipient of Social Security. And, for those receiving Social Security benefits, likely they would only do so for a few years before passing.

Today, the ratio of how many people are in the workforce compared to those utilizing Social Security is approximately about three to one and it's swiftly moving by the end of this decade. By the start of

---

[10] Social Security. 2017. "Retirement Age: Background." https://www.ssa.gov/planners/retire/background.html. Accessed Aug. 2, 2017.

2020, it will be approximately two to one.[11] This story is a way of saying that we're definitely living longer. We mentioned earlier, when we were talking about some of the things to avoid, the fact that we just don't have the pensions anymore. You know, it's not our daddy or granddaddy's retirement program anymore. What I'm getting at is that it is up to us to create our own supplemental stream of lifetime income.

That is typically done in the form of an annuity, as I mentioned earlier in the book. A lot of times, if you Google that up, you'll read that annuities are bad. I do think that some annuities can be bad. Some annuities can be very high in fees, some of them can have long surrender charges, and some have little to no guarantees. .

But there are some very good annuities out there to assist in longevity planning. You know, the second thing we touched upon was a market risk in retirement or even just before retirement.

For those out there who have a lot of money in the stock market and who were planning on retiring in 2008, chances are some of them went back to work for a while or stayed working for a while. One of the worst things that could have happened was that they had already retired in early 2008 and couldn't get their

---

[11] Social Security. 2017. "Social Security History: Ratios." https://www.ssa.gov/history/ratios.html. Accessed Aug. 2, 2017.

job back and couldn't recover from some of the major losses. That's why planning is so important. No one can predict what the market is going to do at any time, and you don't want all your eggs in the market and have a major loss. There aren't a lot of people who can withstand that loss right before retirement.

To illustrate the point I'm trying to make, I'll share a story of someone who *didn't* work with us. A new client came to us and wanted to make sure her retirement was unlike that of her sister. Her sister had retired in January 2007, and this is *her* story.

The sister had a 401(k) since the 70s, according to her sister, and she had been growing and contributing that money pretty consistently. She hadn't really looked much at her statements; they were all moving in a very positive direction.

Well, she had taken a little bit of a hit back in the early 2000s, and it got her thinking about whether her money was too much at risk, but then the market bounced back and she was back at a comfortable level. She thought life was good. She started pulling money out of that particular account, which had great rates of return over the course of time.

She decided to retire early in 2007, and we obviously have one of the biggest market corrections we've ever had shortly after. She had a very high equity portfolio, and she lost immediately over a third of her portfolio because of the market correction. On top of that, she was pulling the money that she needed each and every month out of that particular account.

She's had to change her entire retirement based on the preceding situation. This example is why I can't stress enough that it's very important for someone to sit down with a professional and figure out what their risk tolerance is, and maybe put some principal protection type of moves into place as they get close to or at the point of retirement. We often refer to these times as the "retirement red zone"; the few years just before or just after retirement. They are very important to the prosperity of one's retirement picture.

Folks in this timeframe won't have the time to deal with that rocky part of the mountain, because they don't have that much accumulation time left, or they may have already started the distribution portion of their investment life cycle.

That's a real-life example of someone who did a good job saving, had seen that market continuously go up, but just had not done a very good job when it came to reviewing and sitting down with their advisor. We try to do the flip side of that coin. We want to make sure that we're meeting with our clients, at a minimum, on an annual basis—typically a semi-annual basis, because we want to make sure that we're doing everything we possibly can for them.

We want to make sure that they understand where we're at.

As of the writing of this book, the Dow Jones Industrial Average, just within the last week, reached over 22,000.[12] We're talking at a DOW record number that's at an all-time high, that's pushed that type of growth. It's very important for people to understand the market risk that's associated with the market currently. That's something that we could help our clients with in a big, big way. If we plan properly, we can help them create tax-efficient strategies, we can provide them with insurance products such as annuities that guarantee income, and we can help ensure that they are planning for a very fulfilling retirement.

Another important value we bring to the table, while a vague one at that, is planning; oftentimes planning for the unknown. We talked a little bit about who ends up being the one to carry the responsibility or the burden if there are some major health care or long-term care issues. What happens if Mom and Dad start running out of money in retirement, or if there's just simply a lack of planning, there's not a will in place, and there's not a lot of those types of things covered, and those plans haven't been laid out?

---

[12] Matt Egan. CNN Money. Aug. 2, 2017. "What big fat bubble? Trump cheers as Dow hits 22,000."
http://money.cnn.com/2017/08/02/investing/dow-22000-trump-apple-wall-street/index.html. Accessed Aug. 2, 2017.

That can be very stressful for the next generation; it can be very stressful on the family.

Keep in mind that there are other things out there that can happen along the way. Not just the passing of a family member or an older generation. Many, many things can happen along the way. Making sure that you do take that time to sit down and review your plan with somebody is important because, even if someone has a young family, something like a life insurance contract can be a life saver. We've had to deliver a few death benefit checks, and some of those checks are the only reason that a family can stay in their house. Some of those checks are the only reason that those kids are going to be able to stay in the same neighborhood, the same school. Some of those checks are the only reason that food's going to be able to be put on the table. I find that to be very powerful and a very important step.

Disability income insurance is the same way. If someone is no longer able to work because of a disability or something of the sort; you don't think it's going to happen to me, but we've dealt with those issues over the course of time and it's fulfilling when we know that we've done our job. Those are some examples of some people we've worked with.

Simply the idea of saving can be crucial. A gal came into our office and said, "Hey, I'm going to retire next year. I'm going to start taking Social Security at the age of 62. Here's my retirement plan." She had a little over $40,000 in that retirement plan and that was it. It's awfully tough to retire and to retire happily if you haven't done a little bit of the work along the way. Those pieces need to be covered and they need to be reviewed and they need to be implemented.

So, at our office, we have a set process that we've put in place that we take our clients through. We have something called a Financial Roadmap™, which is a gathering device we use to try to take a bird's eye view of someone's financial picture. What we typically like to do is take an opportunity to introduce ourselves, make sure that it's a good fit for both of us. Introduce a prospective client to this Financial Roadmap™ piece that we use.

As a data-gathering piece, it allows me and my team to get to work on some ideas and some concepts that are tailored to that prospective client.

At that point in time, we use some cutting-edge software when it comes to planning because it's super important to make sure that someone's risk tolerance is proper, to make sure that those goals are aligned. It's important for you to understand the sequence in which you should utilize some of your money. I frequently help clients answer questions like, "Do I use my IRA first or do I use my Roth IRA first? Do I use my bank account money first?" Those pieces are all things that we can help with.

We meet with people; show them how we do business. We gather their information in that Financial Roadmap™. We take some other steps to make sure that we understand someone's risk tolerance. I am especially thorough in making sure that the people I meet with understand what their portfolio could look like in X number of years if they keep doing what they're doing. We also show them what it could look like maybe if they were able to implement a few other ideas.

Everyone is different; everyone is unique. There are a lot of different strategies and financial products out there that can help someone in retirement. A little bit of planning can go a long way.

While there are a lot of minefields to avoid in retirement, one important piece of planning is who you've got on your team. If you have more questions about what we've covered in this book, or want to find out if we'd be a good fit for being part of your financial team, you can check out my firm and our services at **https://rootedretirement.com/.**

There's some information on there about some of the services, as well as some information about myself. Our direct line is 815-918-4727. The toll-free option is 866.766.8332. This is what I do. I help people create a financial plan for uncertain future so they aren't caught off guard and have a retirement that is what they hoped it would be.

Here'sd How to Create Your Retirement Roadmap

We all know we should plan for retirement, but it's easy to get confused with how to plan for an uncertain future. Add in some of the confusing financial terms and products available and it can be a challenge to figure out which road to take or which way to turn.

That's where we come in. We use our Financial Roadmap™ to help people just like you create your own map to retirement, to help you navigate your retirement with confidence.

Step 1: We meet with you in a personalized strategy session to find out what your unique challenges and opportunities with your retirement.

Step 2: From there we help draft your Financial Roadmap™ to develop a plan to make sure to map out what is needed for you to have a successful retirement.

Step 3: We help you implement your Financial Roadmap™ using the appropriate financial vehicles and strategies, and check in with you regularly to ensure the plan is still on course.

Most people put off planning for retirement because they're overwhelmed and they're a little bit frightened by the process.

Now you can go through our painless process that puts things in an easy to understand format so you can easily implement the strategies for a more confident retirement.

If you'd like us to help, send an email to: **ZachGray@RootedRetirement.com** and we'll take it from there.

www.ingramcontent.com/pod-product-compliance
Lightning Source LLC
Chambersburg PA
CBHW050028230526
45470CB00003B/1174